# THE LEADERSHIP DETOUR
# COMPANION GUIDE

## REFLECTION, RECLAMATION, AND REAL-LIFE LEADERSHIP PRACTICE

### DR. TAMMI FLEMING

IILLUSTRATIONS BY DESTINY WHITE

WITH FORMATTING AND EDITORIAL SUPPORT BY EUFEROSE CORREA WHITE

Diamond Consultants, LLC                    Sharon Hill, Pennsylvania

Library of Congress Control Number: 2025914019
ISBN: 979-8-9986680-4-3 (paperback)

Subjects: Leadership—Personal Growth; Executive Coaching; Self-Reflection; Women in Leadership; Career Development
Classification: BUSINESS & ECONOMICS / Leadership; SELF-HELP / Personal Growth / Success
Publication Date: September 18, 2025

This guide is a companion to *The Leadership Detour: How the Unexpected Path Shaped My Success*.

For permissions, inquiries, or bulk orders, contact:
Diamond Consultants, LLC
[diamondconsultantsllc.com]
[info@diamondconsultantsllc.com]

Printed in the United States of America.

Disclaimer: This workbook is not a substitute for therapy, legal advice, or financial guidance. It is a tool for self-reflection and professional development.

*Dedication*

For every leader

who has ever questioned whether they belonged-

You do.

You always did.

This is your reclamation.

## *Acknowledgments*

Thank you to every reader who joined The Leadership Detour journey early. This companion guide was created with you in mind—as a thank-you, a roadmap, and a declaration that your leadership matters.

*A Note from Dr. Tammi:*

**Welcome to The Leadership Detour Companion Guide!**

This workbook is your space to pause, reflect, and take ownership of your leadership journey.

Each chapter mirrors the structure of the book and includes:

- A Purpose Statement to ground your reflections

- Guided Reflection Prompts to surface internal beliefs and past experiences

- Awareness Checks or Reclaiming Activities to increase insight

- Integration Practices to apply lessons in real time

- A Coaching Prompt to stretch your thinking and invite transformation

There's no rush. You don't need perfect answers. This guide is designed to meet you wherever you are and grow with you. Use it at your own pace, alone or in community. Come back to it when you need clarity, courage, or a reset.

Before you begin each section:

- Give yourself time and space.

- Be honest with yourself—this is for you.

- Use a journal, voice notes, or the margins of this workbook—whatever feels natural.

This is more than a workbook. It's a coaching companion—a space to reconnect with your values, voice, and vision.

# GUIDE TO SYMBOLS AND ANT STORY

Throughout this companion guide, you'll find hand-drawn icons designed to help you navigate your reflection and coaching journey. Each one represents a unique type of prompt—from grounding questions to real-world integration tools.

These illustrations are more than decoration—they're invitations. Symbols that help you slow down, look inward, and move forward with clarity and courage.

One icon in particular may catch your eye: the ant. We chose the ant because of what it represents—**resilience, purpose, and collective strength**. Ants may be small, but they are powerful when in motion. They build, they lead, and they always find a way forward. Much like leaders who reclaim their voice.

Destiny White, the artist behind each symbol, brought these icons to life with intention and care. Use them as a visual rhythm throughout the guide—as pause points, turning points, and quiet reminders of your leadership detour.

# GUIDE TO SYMBOLS AND ANT STORY

| | | |
|---|---|---|
| | **The Ant**<br>*Legacy & Consistency* | A symbol of strength, collaboration, and steady leadership. The ant reminds us that impact is built over time. |
| | **Thought Bubble with Question Mark**<br>*Coaching Questions* | Designed to challenge your thinking and reveal deeper insights as you lead from within. |
| | **Two Puzzle Pieces**<br>*Integration Practices* | Prompts and practices to help you bridge reflection with action and apply insights in your leadership. |
| | **Megaphone with Mouth**<br>*Voice & Visibility* | Invitations to consider how you use your voice, take up space, and influence others with presence and authenticity. |
| | **Hand with Pencil**<br>*Journaling & Reflection* | Prompts for self-inquiry, truth-telling, and deep personal exploration. |

# THE ANT PATH:
# A DETOUR WITH PURPOSE

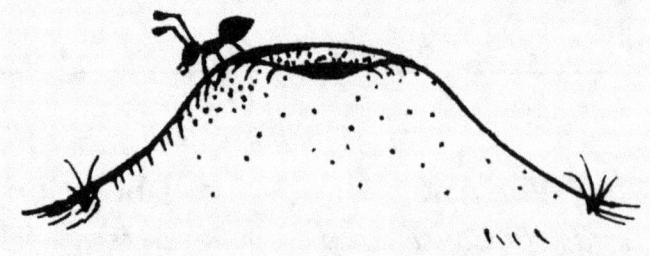

## ANTS ARE AMONG THE SMALLEST CREATURES—BUT THEIR MOVEMENTS REVEAL SOMETHING PROFOUND ABOUT LEADERSHIP.

  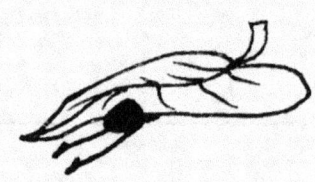

When an obstacle blocks their path, ants don't stop. They don't panic. They pause, reassess, and reroute. They'll detour—over a rock, around a puddle, under a leaf—until they find a new way forward. Their power isn't in brute force. It's in persistence, adaptability, and collective intelligence. Leadership is much the same.

Your journey may not follow a straight line. Detours—whether caused by setbacks, self-doubt, or systems—aren't proof you're lost. They're proof you're still moving. Like the ant, you pause. Reassess. And find another way.

Detours don't delay destiny—they often define it. They sharpen your vision, build resilience, and deepen your leadership presence. So the next time you feel off track, remember the ant. Tiny. Relentless. Strategic. And always willing to take the long way—if that's the path that leads forward.

# TABLE OF CONTENTS:

# CHAPTER 1
## YOUR STARTING POINT

*"Self-awareness is not about perfection. It's about reflection, recognition, and the choice to evolve."*

—Dr. Tammi Fleming

# PURPOSE OF THIS CHAPTER

Every leadership journey has a beginning—and it often starts long before the job titles or accolades. This chapter invites you to look back with intention and compassion, exploring the early moments, people, and beliefs that formed your leadership identity. The goal isn't to dwell on the past, but to reclaim it as a source of power, wisdom, and clarity.

## How to Begin This Chapter

Before diving into the prompts, take a quiet moment. Breathe. Reflect on your earliest memories of responsibility, influence, or voice. You're not just recalling your past—you're uncovering the origin story of your leadership. Start from a place of curiosity, not judgment.

# GUIDED REFLECTION

Who was the first person you saw as a leader—not by title, but by presence, impact, or influence?

_____

What did they do that made others pay attention?

_____

_____

_____

_____

_____

What early leadership strengths showed up in your life?

_____

Were these leadership strengths celebrated, misunderstood, or ignored?

_____

_____

_____

_____

Did you view others- especially peers- as competition or as mirrors?

_____

What did that reveal about your sense of worth and belonging?

_____

_____

_____

_____

Who were the unsung heroes in your life—those individuals who saw your potential before you did?

_____

What did they offer you that still lives in your leadership today?

_____

_____

_____

_____

# ACTIVITY: WRITE A LETTER

**Why this matters:**

Sometimes growth requires a conversation we never got to have. This letter-writing activity helps you reflect on an early relationship that shaped your sense of leadership—positively or painfully. It's an exercise in **closure**, **clarity**, and **compassion**.

## Your Practice

Write a letter to someone who challenged you early in your journey—someone you may have envied, misunderstood, or learned from. This letter is for your eyes only.

### Use these questions to guide your writing:

- What would you say to them now, with the self-awareness you've gained?

- What do you now understand about them—or about yourself—that you couldn't see then?

- What healing, clarity, or insight might this letter unlock for you?

- You don't have to send it. But write it. There's power in your voice—even when it's written just for you.

(You'll find space on the next page to write.)

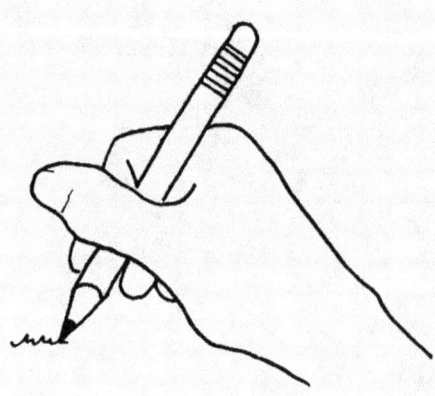

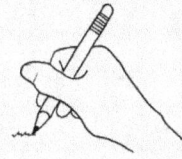

# ACTIVITY: WRITE A LETTER

_____

_____

_____

_____

_____

_____

_____

_____

_____

_____

_____

_____

_____

_____

_____

_____

*"You don't need a perfect beginning to become an extraordinary leader."*

—Dr. Tammi Fleming

# COACHING PROMPT

# RECLAIMING THE POWER OF YOUR STORY

It's easy to underestimate the early chapters of our lives, especially if they felt messy, painful, or unfinished. But those moments often hold our deepest leadership wisdom—if we're willing to see them differently.

**Reflect:**

What part of your story have you been underestimating, hiding, or overlooking... that actually shaped your greatest leadership gift?

Take a moment to write your response.
Let your answer flow without editing or censoring. You're not writing for perfection—you're writing for clarity and connection.

# COACHING PROMPT

_____
_____
_____
_____
_____
_____
_____
_____
_____
_____
_____
_____
_____
_____
_____
_____

# CHAPTER 2
## RECLAIMING THE RIGHT TO BELONG

*"When you show up whole, you offer others the permission to do the same."*

—Dr. Tammi Fleming

# PURPOSE OF THIS CHAPTER

This section invites you to pause and examine the early messages—spoken or unspoken—that shaped how you navigate leadership spaces. It's about noticing the ways you've adjusted to belong and choosing which adjustments still serve you—and which ones you're ready to release

## How to Begin This Chapter

Before diving into the prompts, take a breath and center yourself. Think about a time when you felt like you didn't quite fit—but still had to lead. This chapter is your space to name what you've had to quiet or shift just to be taken seriously—and to decide what you want to reclaim moving forward.

 **GUIDED REFLECTION**

What is one word, phrase, or habit from your upbringing that you've edited or hidden in professional spaces?

_____

Why did you feel the need to change or conceal it?

_____

_____

_____

_____

How do you feel about it now?

_____

_____

_____

_____

_____

_____

Think of a time when someone questioned your style, voice, or presence.

_____

How did it affect the way you showed up afterward?

_____

_____

_____

_____

What, if anything, did you change about yourself?

_____

_____

_____

_____

When did you first realize that fitting in might come at the cost of authenticity?

_____

Did that realization shift your behavior or beliefs about belonging?

_____

_____

_____

_____

# ACTIVITY: AWARENESS CHECK

## HOW HAVE YOU BEEN ADJUSTING TO FIT IN?

Before we can reclaim our full presence, we have to see where—and why—we've been dimming or editing ourselves. Many of us have unconsciously made subtle shifts in order to feel accepted or avoid being judged.

This activity helps you name the places where adaptation may have turned into self-erasure. You're not blaming yourself. You're simply becoming more aware—so you can choose more consciously going forward.

Circle any of the ways you've adjusted yourself at work (past or present):

- My wardrobe or style

- My natural speech or accent

- The way I express emotions

- What I share about my background

- How often I speak in meetings

- My tone or vocabulary

- How much space I take up
  (literally or metaphorically)

> **Self-erasure:** The act of minimizing, suppressing, or abandoning parts of your identity, voice, or truth in order to be accepted, survive, or succeed in environments that feel unsafe, biased, or unreceptive.
>
> Self-erasure can show up as downplaying your accomplishments, withholding opinions, silencing emotion, or conforming to norms that don't reflect your authentic self. In leadership, self-erasure is often a survival response—but healing and growth begin when we name it, interrupt it, and begin to lead with our full presence.

**Now ask yourself:**

*Which of these adjustments were strategic—and which were rooted in fear, pressure, or survival?*

As a way to ground this reflection, write a one-sentence declaration of what you're reclaiming today. Let it be bold, honest, and written for you:

I no longer shrink _____ just to fit in.

From now on, I will _____.

# INTEGRATION PRACTICE:

## RECLAIMING IN REAL TIME

**Awareness is powerful—but it's not enough on its own.**

This next section helps you take small but meaningful steps to practice leading from your full, authentic self. There are three integration activities:

1. Voice Reclamation
2. Style Reclamation
3. Boundary Affirmation

These aren't performative actions—they're reclamation rituals that reconnect you to your voice, your style, and your truth.

Choose one to begin with. Or try all three over the next week. What matters most is intention, not perfection.

# INTEGRATION PRACTICE

## VOICE RECLAMATION

**Why this matters:**
Many of us have unconsciously edited the way we speak—abandoning words, phrases, or intonations from our upbringing to appear more "professional." This exercise helps you reclaim your voice and honor the roots of your communication style.

### Your Practice

- Choose a phrase, word, or saying from your upbringing that you've stopped using in professional spaces.
- Say it aloud.
- Reflect on how it feels in your body.

Now write a short paragraph using that phrase. (No edits—just voice.)

_____

_____

_____

_____

_____

_____

# INTEGRATION PRACTICE

## STYLE RECLAMATION

**Why this matters:**
Leadership isn't just about strategy—it's about presence. What you wear is part of how you take up space. This practice invites you to embody your culture, creativity, or energy through style—not as performance, but as a form of alignment.

### Your Practice

- Wear something this week that reflects your heritage, creativity, or energy.
- Take a picture.
- Journal: How did it feel to lead from a place of alignment?

_____

_____

_____

_____

_____

_____

_____

**PLACE PICTURE HERE**

# INTEGRATION PRACTICE

## BOUNDARY AFFIRMATION

**Why this matters:**
Reclaiming your presence isn't just visual or verbal—it's internal. This simple affirmation helps reset your mindset and prepare you to lead from power, not performance.

### Your Practice

- Before your next meeting, practice saying aloud:

*"I don't need to shrink to lead."*

- Say it until it feels like truth.
- Then act from that truth.

**Note any reflections from this integration practice:**

_____

_____

_____

_____

# COACHING PROMPT

# STANDING IN YOUR POWER

You've reflected. You've reclaimed. You've practiced showing up more fully. Now, let's imagine what's possible when you lead without editing or shrinking—when your presence becomes a power move, not a performance.

What would it look like to walk into your next leadership space not hoping to blend in—but choosing to stand out, on purpose, in power, and without apology?

Reflect on the following questions:

- How would you walk in?

- What would you say or do differently?

- What energy would you bring into the room?

- How would it feel in your body to lead without apology?

Now, take a moment to write your vision for that moment on the following page:

Write answers on next page:

# COACHING PROMPT

How would you walk in?

_____

_____

_____

What would you say or do differently?

_____

_____

_____

What energy would you bring into the room?

_____

_____

_____

How would it feel in your body to lead without apology?

_____

_____

_____

_____

# CHAPTER 3
## CLOSING THE LEADERSHIP GAP

*"What got you here may not be enough to get you there."*

—Dr. Tammi Fleming

# PURPOSE OF THIS CHAPTER

This chapter explores the turning point many leaders face: the moment when being technically excellent is no longer enough. It's where identity, perception, and presence begin to matter more than checklists or credentials. This chapter invites you to reflect on your first leadership detour—when your growth required more than hard work, and you had to step into a new version of yourself.

## How to Begin This Chapter

Take a deep breath and think about a moment when you felt stuck, misread, or overlooked—even though you knew you were performing well. This chapter asks you to reflect honestly on that experience, not to dwell, but to identify what shifted or needed to shift. You're not just recalling a challenge—you're reclaiming the insight and wisdom it gave you.

# GUIDED REFLECTION

When did you first feel like your career was stalling—despite strong performance?

_____

What did you tell yourself at the time?

_____

_____

_____

_____

How did it feel emotionally?

_____

_____

_____

_____

_____

_____

_____

_____

_____

_____

Have you ever been viewed as "the expert" but not the leader?

_____

What signals were you receiving that you may have missed or misunderstood?

_____

_____

_____

_____

What's your relationship to feedback and how others perceive you?

_____

Have you ever questioned how others were experiencing your leadership?

_____

_____

_____

_____

How do you typically approach relationships in your professional life?

_____

Would you describe yourself as more task-focused or connection-focused?

_____

_____

_____

_____

How might that tendency shape the way others experience your leadership presence?

_____

_____

_____

_____

_____

_____

# ACTIVITY:
# REWRITE THE ROOM

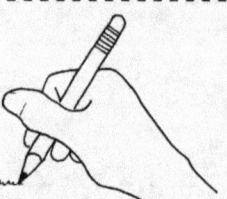

**Why this matters:**

Leadership isn't just about what you do—it's about how you show up. This practice invites you to reframe your mindset and shift your presence in a real-world setting. Small shifts in energy, tone, and connection can have powerful ripple effects.

### Your Practice
### Intentional Leadership in Action:

**Step 1:**

Identify a real space where you can practice showing up differently. This could be a team meeting, 1:1 check-in, strategy session, or even a community conversation.

The meeting or event I'm choosing:

Date and time:

**Step 2:**

Choose one or more intentional actions to try.
Check the box next to the action(s) you commit to practicing during your selected meeting or event:

☐ Arrive early and ask someone about their day.

☐ Follow up on something personal a colleague shared.

☐ Listen for tone and body language—not just words.

☐ Shift your internal script: *What are you telling yourself before you walk in?*

**Step 3:**
After the event or meeting, take a moment to reflect:
What changed when you led with presence instead of perfection?

_____

_____

_____

_____

_____

_____

_____

_____

_____

_____

_____

_____

_____

_____

_____

_____

# VISUAL ACTIVITY: PERCEPTION VS INTENTION MAP

Sometimes there's a difference between how we intend to show up and how we're actually perceived. This activity will help you uncover and close those gaps, so your leadership presence aligns with your true intentions.

### Instructions:

Review the examples in the two columns below. Then, complete the remaining rows with your own real-life examples of how your intentions may be misinterpreted. Be honest-this is for your growth, not for judgement.

| My Intention | How I May Be Perceived |
|---|---|
| • "I want to be seen as helpful" | • "I may come across as controlling" |
| • "I stay quiet to respect space" | • "I seem disengaged or disinterested" |
| • "I'm focused on results" | • "I might seem cold or distant" |
| • | • |
| • | • |
| • | • |

### Next Steps:

Circle one mismatch that stands out to you.

Reflect in the space below:

What small shift in behavior or communication could help close the perception vs. intention gap?

_____

_____

_____

_____

_____

_____

_____

_____

_____

_____

_____

_____

_____

_____

_____

_____

# COACHING PROMPT

# LEADING WITH PRESENCE, NOT PERFORMANCE

Sometimes, the real gap isn't between you and the next level—it's between who you've been and who you're becoming. This prompt is about stepping fully into that new version of yourself, even before you feel ready.

**What if the next level of your leadership isn't about doing more—but about becoming more?**

What part of your leadership identity are you being invited to evolve?

**Journal Prompt:**

- What would it look like to show up this week not as "the expert," but as the leader?

- How would your presence shift if you released perfection and focused on connection?

# COACHING PROMPT

1.) What would it look like to show up this week not as "the expert," but as the leader?

_____

_____

_____

_____

_____

_____

_____

2.) How would your presence shift if you released perfection and focused on connection?

_____

_____

_____

_____

_____

_____

_____

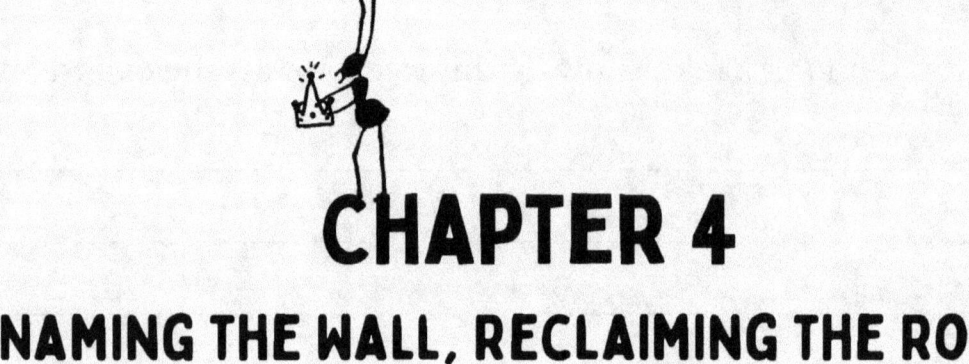

# CHAPTER 4
## NAMING THE WALL, RECLAIMING THE ROOM

*"Your plateau isn't a dead end—it's a mirror."*

—Dr. Tammi Fleming

# PURPOSE OF THIS CHAPTER

This chapter explores the often-unspoken moment when high performers hit a wall—not because they've failed, but because they've outgrown the strategies that once worked. Here, we reflect on that plateau, examine how voice and visibility shape leadership perception, and begin the work of rewriting your narrative from a place of honesty and evolution.

## How to Begin This Chapter

Before diving in, take a deep breath and release the pressure to have it all figured out. You may be navigating a personal or professional transition, or simply sensing a misalignment that's hard to name. This section invites you to name your wall—not as a weakness, but as a signal. A mirror. An invitation.

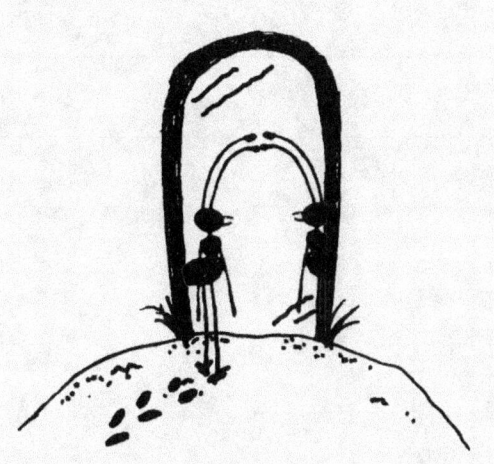

# GUIDED REFLECTION

### YOUR LEADERSHIP PLATEAU

Where in your professional life do you feel stuck, stagnant, or no longer growing?

_____

_____

Are you working harder without seeing better results?

_____

_____

How is your presence being received—and how are you interpreting that feedback?

_____

_____

_____

_____

## VOICE & BELONGING

Have you ever felt like your voice—literally or metaphorically—was too much or not enough?

_____

What comments, feedback, or interactions shaped your relationship with how you speak, show up, or express yourself?

_____

_____

_____

_____

_____

_____

_____

_____

_____

_____

_____

_____

## THE MYTH OF ARRIVAL

Have you experienced a career "arrival" that didn't feel the way you expected it to?

_____

What were you hoping would change with the new title or opportunity—and what actually did?

_____

_____

_____

_____

_____

How have those moments shaped your definition of leadership today?

_____

_____

_____

_____

_____

_____

_____

# ACTIVITY 1:
# REWRITE YOUR PROFESSIONAL NARRATIVE

**Why this matters:**

Sometimes what keeps us stuck isn't the situation—it's the story we're telling ourselves about it. This exercise invites you to step out of performance mode and into radical honesty. It's a first step in reclaiming your voice and power.

### Your Practice

Set a timer for 10–15 minutes and write freely using this prompt:

*"If I'm honest, the real reason I feel stuck right now is..."*

Let your voice be unfiltered. Don't edit. Don't worry about structure. Let the truth flow.

(You'll find space on the next page to write.)

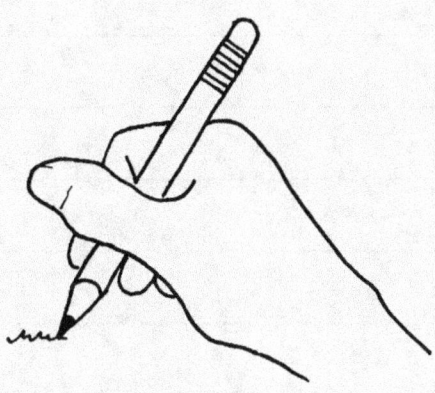

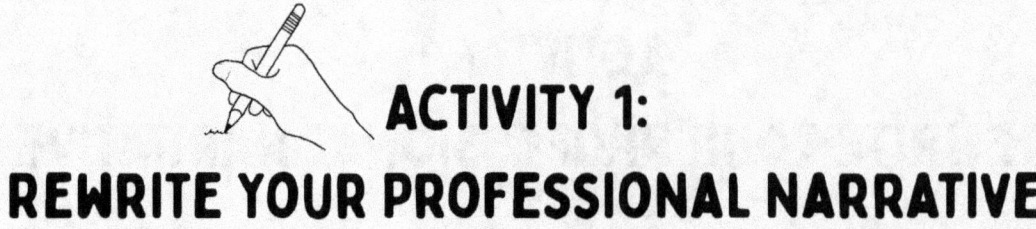

# ACTIVITY 1:
# REWRITE YOUR PROFESSIONAL NARRATIVE

*"If I'm honest, the real reason I feel stuck right now is…"*

_____

_____

_____

_____

_____

_____

_____

_____

_____

_____

_____

_____

_____

_____

_____

_____

_____

_____

_____

_____

_____

_____

_____

_____

## After you write

Re-read what you wrote.
Highlight any fears, assumptions, or expectations that are ready to be challenged.

## Now answer

*"What would it look like to lead myself forward from here?"*

_____

_____

_____

_____

_____

_____

_____

# ACTIVITY 2:
# PLATEAU AWARENESS PATTERNS

**Why this matters:**

Hitting a wall in your career isn't always about failure—it's often about repetition. When high performers plateau, it's usually because they've outgrown strategies that once worked. This activity helps you name the patterns that might be keeping you stuck, so you can make space for what's next.

## Your Practice

Review the four common triggers that contribute to leadership plateaus.

1. Being known only for your technical skills.
2. Lack of feedback or unclear expectations.
3. Feeling pressure to perform, not lead.
4. Losing connection to purpose or values.

In the table (on the next page), reflect on whether you've experienced any or all of the triggers and describe what it looked or felt like in your professional journey.

| Common Plateau Trigger | Have you Experienced This? | | What did it look or feel like? |
| --- | --- | --- | --- |
| Being known only for your technical skills | Yes | No | |
| Lack of feedback or unclear expectations | Yes | No | |
| Feeling pressure to perform, not lead | Yes | No | |
| Losing connection to purpose or values | Yes | No | |

# ACTIVITY 2:
# PLATEAU AWARENESS PATTERNS

## Follow-Up Reflection

After reviewing your responses, take a moment to reflect:

1.) Which of these plateau triggers shows up most often for you—and what might be underneath it?

2.) What assumptions, fears, or expectations might be reinforcing this cycle?

_____

_____

_____

_____

_____

_____

_____

_____

_____

_____

_____

_____

# COACHING PROMPT

# HONESTY AS A LEADERSHIP PRACTICE

When we stop hiding behind performance and start telling the truth, we unlock a different kind of power—one rooted in alignment, clarity, and self-leadership.

**Journal Prompt:**

- **What story have you been telling yourself about your leadership plateau —and what new story are you ready to write?**

Let this be unfiltered. You're not writing for anyone else-this is for you.

_____

_____

_____

_____

_____

_____

_____

# CHAPTER 5:
## THE BREAKTHROUGH

*"Breakthrough doesn't happen when the world changes. It happens when you do."*

—Dr. Tammi Fleming

# PURPOSE OF THIS CHAPTER

Breakthrough leadership doesn't come from changing the environment—it comes from changing how you show up in it. This chapter invites you to explore the internal shifts that create external momentum: from perfectionism to presence, from reaction to calibration, from isolation to intentional support. You'll reflect on the power of coaching, the difference between mentoring and advice, and what it means to build a leadership circle rooted in growth—not performance.

## How to Begin This Chapter

Think back to a moment where you felt stuck—not because you weren't working hard, but because something deeper needed to shift. This chapter isn't just about surviving challenges—it's about identifying the habits, mindsets, and support systems that help you break through them.

*Give yourself permission to be honest. The breakthrough begins there.*

# GUIDED REFLECTION

## THE COACHING SHIFT

What have you been trying to "perform" your way through in leadership?

_____

_____

_____

_____

_____

How might that shift if you approached it with openness instead of over-preparedness?

_____

_____

_____

_____

_____

## FIXED VS. GROWTH MINDSET

Where in your leadership do you focus more on *looking competent* than *becoming capable*?

_____

_____

_____

What challenge might you be labeling as "personal" that's actually an opportunity for growth?

_____

_____

_____

## SUPPORT SYSTEMS & MENTORSHIP

Who do you turn to when leadership gets heavy?

_____

_____

_____

What role do they play—the Mirror (reflecting truth back to you), the Key (unlocking new perspectives or opportunities), or the Anchor (keeping you grounded)?

_____

_____

## VOICE & CALIBRATION

Think of a recent situation where you held back your truth.

_____

_____

_____

What would it have sounded like to calibrate instead of collapse or confront?

_____

_____

_____

_____

_____

_____

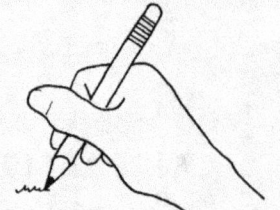

# AWARENESS ACTIVITY:
# BUILD YOUR LEADERSHIP SUPPORT CIRCLE

**Why this matters:**

Growth requires more than effort—it requires the right people in your corner. This activity helps you map out your personal board of directors, based on the roles that nurture transformation, not just performance.

### Your Practice

Use the table below to reflect on who currently plays these roles in your life—and where you might have gaps.

| Role | Description | Who fits this role? |
|------|-------------|---------------------|
| Mirror | Reflects your patterns, blind spots, and behaviors with clarity and care | |
| Key | Challenges your thinking, reframes your mindset, opens new paths of growth | |
| Anchor | Grounds you emotionally and reminds you who you are when you feel off-balance | |

# JOURNAL PROMPT:
# WHO'S IN YOUR CIRCLE?

"If I built my Leadership Support Circle based on who grows me—not just who knows me—it would include..."

_____

_____

_____

_____

_____

# ACTION STEP:
# CREATE IT

- Identify 2–3 people who fit the Mirror, Key, or Anchor roles.

- Reach out—set an intention for the relationship.

- Plan a quarterly check-in using one of these prompts:

  - "What's shifted in my leadership?"
  - "Where am I growing—and where do I need challenge?"

**Notes:**

_____

_____

_____

_____

# COACHING PROMPT

## OPEN IS THE NEW STRONG

You don't have to have all the answers. You don't have to stay polished to stay powerful. Being open—to reflection, feedback, and growth—is one of the most courageous leadership moves you can make.

Journal:

- **What have you been resisting that might actually be the doorway to your breakthrough?**

_____

_____

_____

_____

_____

# RECLAIMING YOUR VOICE

**Coaching Prompt**

What part of your voice have you been holding back?

- How do you modulate or mute your tone, volume, or authenticity in professional settings?

- When was the last time you felt fully free to speak without editing yourself?

# RECLAIMING YOUR VOICE

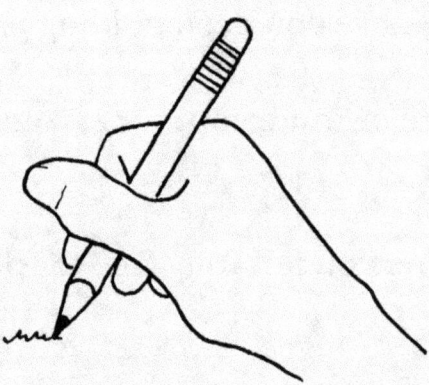

**Voice Reclamation Challenge:**

Write a short paragraph as your unedited self—no corporate polish, no filtering. Use your real tone, rhythm, and truth.

Then read it out loud. Hear yourself again.

_____

_____

_____

_____

_____

_____

_____

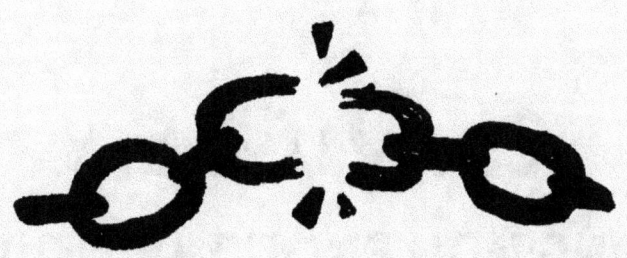

## YOUR BREAKTHROUGH STATEMENT

### Complete this statement to close your workbook session:

*"The next version of my leadership will require me to*

*let go of* _____ *and reclaim* _____ *"*

# CHAPTER 6
## LEADING WITH EMOTIONAL TRUTH

*"Emotional intelligence is not about being unshaken. It's about being aware, responsive, and rooted in who you are—even when the room tells you to be someone else."*

—Dr. Tammi Fleming

# PURPOSE OF THIS CHAPTER

This chapter invites you to examine the internal shifts that happen when you lead with emotional honesty. Too often, we confuse composure with control or silence with strategy. Mastering emotional intelligence means moving beyond emotional suppression and toward emotional presence. You'll reflect on how emotions inform your leadership, how you respond in high-stakes moments, and how to align your internal state with the values and influence you want to carry.

## How to Begin This Chapter

Start by pausing. Think about a recent moment when you felt something strongly—frustration, anger, fear, joy—and didn't express it. What was the setting? What did you do instead of naming the emotion? What story did you tell yourself about what it meant to "stay professional"?

Before diving into the activities, revisit the "Three Stories" coaching tool if needed (Page 60). This chapter asks you to slow down, sit with your emotional patterns, and give yourself permission to feel—without judgment.

Be honest. Be curious. You're not fixing anything here—you're noticing. That's where emotional power begins.

# EMOTIONAL INTELLIGENCE IN ACTION

## EMOTIONAL AUDIT

What emotion has been showing up most in your work life lately?

_____

Where do you feel it in your body?

_____

What thoughts are typically attached to that emotion?

_____

_____

_____

_____

What do you usually do in response?

_____

_____

_____

# THE "THREE STORIES" REFLECTION

Think back to a recent difficult interaction. Answer the following:

What was the **story you told yourself** about what happened?

_____

_____

_____

_____

What's a **story the other person might tell?**

_____

_____

_____

_____

What's a possible **truth in the middle?**

_____

_____

_____

Now answer:

What emotions came up during or after that interaction?

_____

_____

_____

_____

Where did you feel those emotions in your body?

_____

_____

_____

_____

How did those emotions shape your behavior or silence your voice?

_____

_____

_____

# THE FIVE DOMAINS CHECK-IN

**Self-Awareness:**
What's a recent moment you didn't notice how you were feeling until after the fact?

_____

_____

_____

_____

_____

**Self-Regulation:**
How did you manage (or not manage) your reaction?

_____

_____

_____

_____

**Motivation:**
Are your current goals aligned with your values?

_____

_____

_____

_____

**Empathy:**
When did you last pause to consider someone else's emotional state?

_____

_____

_____

_____

**Social Skills:**
What's one thing you could do to build trust this week?

_____

_____

_____

_____

# FIVE DOMAINS SELF-CHECK

**Self-Awareness:**
What helps you notice what you feel before you react?

_____

_____

_____

_____

_____

**Self-Regulation:**
When was the last time you chose to respond with care instead of react out of habit?

_____

_____

_____

_____

**Motivation:**
What's currently driving your work—fear, purpose, or proof?

_____

_____

_____

_____

**Empathy:**
Who in your life needs you to see them more fully right now?

_____

_____

_____

_____

**Social Skills:**
How does your presence affect the spaces you enter?

_____

_____

_____

_____

# 30-DAY PRACTICE COMMITMENT

Choose one domain to focus on. Write your intention below:

Self-Awareness          Self-Regulation          Motivation

Empathy                    Social Skills

My focus domain is: _____

My daily practice or prompt will be:

_____

_____

_____

_____

_____

At the end of 30 days, I want to feel or experience:

_____

*Reminder: This is not about perfection. It's about practicing presence, awareness, and intention—one moment at a time.*

# DAY 1

_____

_____

_____

_____

# DAY 2

_____

_____

_____

_____

# DAY 3

_____

_____

_____

_____

# DAY 4

_____

_____

_____

_____

# DAY 5

_____

_____

_____

_____

# DAY 6

_____

_____

_____

_____

# DAY 7

_____
_____
_____
_____

# DAY 8

_____
_____
_____
_____

# DAY 9

_____
_____
_____
_____

# DAY 10

_____

_____

_____

_____

# DAY 11

_____

_____

_____

_____

# DAY 12

_____

_____

_____

_____

# DAY 13

_____

_____

_____

_____

# DAY 14

_____

_____

_____

_____

# DAY 15

_____

_____

_____

_____

## DAY 16

_____

_____

_____

_____

## DAY 17

_____

_____

_____

_____

## DAY 18

_____

_____

_____

_____

# DAY 19

_____

_____

_____

_____

# DAY 20

_____

_____

_____

_____

# DAY 21

_____

_____

_____

_____

# DAY 22

_____

_____

_____

_____

# DAY 23

_____

_____

_____

_____

# DAY 24

_____

_____

_____

_____

# DAY 25

_____

_____

_____

_____

# DAY 26

_____

_____

_____

_____

# DAY 27

_____

_____

_____

_____

## DAY 28

_____

_____

_____

_____

## DAY 29

_____

_____

_____

_____

## DAY 30

_____

_____

_____

_____

# CHAPTER 7
## LEAD LIKE YOU KNOW YOU BELONG

*"Presence isn't how loud you speak—it's how fully you show up."*

—Dr. Tammi Fleming

# PURPOSE OF THIS CHAPTER

This chapter is about reclaiming executive presence—not as performance, but as alignment. You'll challenge outdated myths about what presence looks like, and you'll reflect on the three core dimensions of presence: your voice, your visibility, and your vibe. The goal isn't to be the loudest in the room—it's to be the most anchored, the most intentional, and the most aligned with who you are.

## How to Begin This Chapter

Presence starts with noticing—how you see yourself, how others experience you, and how energy moves when you enter a space.

Begin by reflecting on this:

- What rooms do you enter silently, even though you have something to say?

- Where are you shrinking—physically, vocally, or energetically?

- What would it feel like to bring your full self into those spaces?

This chapter is designed to guide you from **internal doubt to embodied confidence**, helping you align your inner voice with your outer presence.

# ACTIVITY 1:
# VOICE CHECK — WHERE DO YOU HOLD BACK?

Think about a recent conversation, meeting, or decision point where you stayed silent. Reflect on:

- What did you want to say?

- What stopped you from saying it?

- What story did you tell yourself about staying silent?

### Your Practice

Now complete this sentence:

"If I had trusted my voice, I would have..."

_____

_____

_____

_____

_____

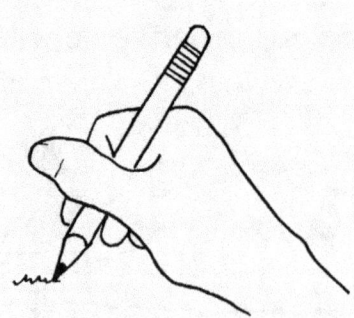

# ACTIVITY 2:
# RECLAIMING VISIBILITY

Think of a space where you've been shrinking—professionally or personally.

Reflect on the following:

- What are you afraid people might think if you took up more space?

- What would it look like to show up fully aligned—without shrinking or deferring?

- What do you want people to feel, know, or remember about you in that space?

## Your Practice

Now complete this sentence:

"The version of me I'm becoming shows up by..."

_____

_____

_____

_____

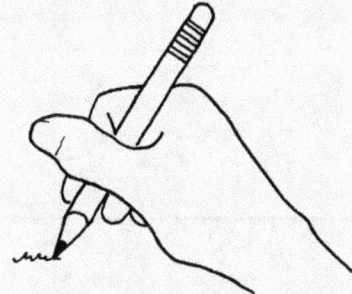

## ACTIVITY 3:
# PRESENCE MAPPING — VOICE, VISIBILITY, VIBE

Using the three-part model (Voice, Visibility, Vibe), complete the prompts below:

| Voice | *Where do I speak with clarity and calm? Where do I trail off or second-guess myself?* |
|---|---|
| | |

| Visibility | *Where do I allow myself to be seen, and where do I wait to be invited?* |
|---|---|
| | |

| Vibe | *What energy do I bring into the room—and what do I want to leave behind?* |
|------|-----------------------------------------------------------------------|
|      |                                                                       |

**Notes:**

_____

_____

_____

_____

_____

_____

_____

# ACTIVITY 4:
# POWER PRACTICE — SMALL ACTS OF CONFIDENCE

Pick one small, intentional act of executive presence to practice this week. Choose from the list below or write your own:

- Speak up once in a meeting where you'd normally stay silent

- Introduce yourself confidently without minimizing your title or role

- Ask one clarifying or thought-provoking question

- Take the central seat at a meeting table

- Breathe before responding in a tense moment

- Wear something that reflects your style—not just the expected norm

- 

After your practice:

- What shifted in the room—or in you?

- What would it look like to repeat this act of confidence consistently?

_____

_____

_____

_____

# CHAPTER 8
## CLARITY AS COMPASS

*"Clarity turns confusion into conviction. It's not about the path—it's about the permission to walk it."*

—Dr. Tammi Fleming

# PURPOSE OF THIS CHAPTER:

This chapter is designed to help you pause long enough to listen to your inner compass. It will guide you in exploring the kind of leadership you want to embody—not just in your next role, but over the next five years and beyond. Through a series of clarity-centered reflections and alignment-based practices, you'll begin crafting a leadership vision rooted in purpose, not pressure.

## <u>How to Begin This Chapter</u>

This chapter builds on everything that came before it. You've done the work of reclaiming your voice, examining your beliefs, and tuning in to your truth. Now, you'll begin integrating that insight into a sustainable leadership mindset.

Before you begin:

- Give yourself time and stillness. This chapter is meant to stretch over several days.

- Revisit earlier reflections—especially around voice, values, and presence.

- This is not about planning every detail. It's about giving yourself permission to move with intention.

- Each activity in this chapter builds on the last. Trust the process and pace yourself.

# ACTIVITY 1:
# CLARIFY YOUR CURRENT STATE

Take 10–15 minutes to reflect and journal your honest answer to these questions:

- What feels clear in your leadership right now?

- Where are you second-guessing yourself?

- What "shoulds" are you carrying that no longer fit who you're becoming?

**1.) What feels clear in your leadership right now?**

_____

_____

_____

_____

_____

_____

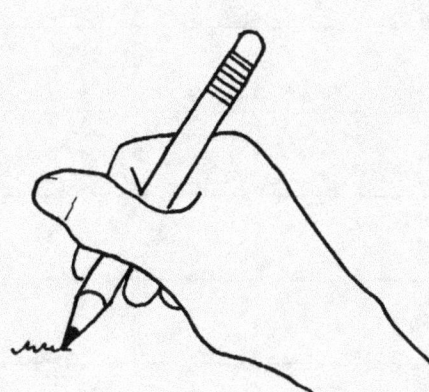

**2.) Where are you second-guessing yourself?**

_____

_____

_____

_____

_____

**3.) What "shoulds" are you carrying that no longer fit who you're becoming?**

_____

_____

_____

_____

_____

_____

_____

_____

_____

_____

# ACTIVITY 2:
# THE ALIGNMENT FILTER

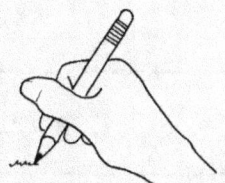

Create a two-column list:

- In one column, list the leadership decisions you've made in the past year.

- In the second, note whether each decision was made from clarity or fear. Be honest.

Then ask: What patterns do you see? What do you want to shift?

| Leadership Decisions | Notes |
|---|---|
|  |  |
|  |  |
|  |  |
|  |  |

| Leadership Decisions | Notes |
| --- | --- |
|  |  |
|  |  |
|  |  |
|  |  |
|  |  |
|  |  |
|  |  |

# ACTIVITY 3:
# WRITE YOUR 5-YEAR LEADERSHIP VISION STATEMENT

Use the reflection prompts from the book (Page 225) to craft a 3–5 sentence vision statement. Think about who you want to be, how you want to feel, and what legacy you want to leave. This isn't about goals—it's about alignment. Include:

- Your core values

- The impact you want to make

- The way you want to show up in the world

_____

_____

_____

_____

_____

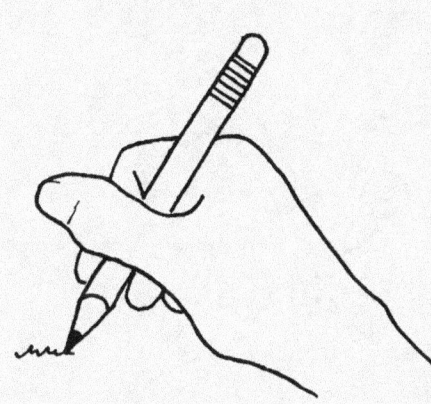

# ACTIVITY 4:
# THE CLARITY CONTRACT

Create a personal "Clarity Contract" to return to when fear or doubt resurfaces. Write down:

- Three truths you've learned about yourself

- Two boundaries you will honor to stay aligned

- One decision you commit to making from clarity, not fear

Sign it. Date it. Keep it somewhere visible.

(You'll find space on the next page to write.)

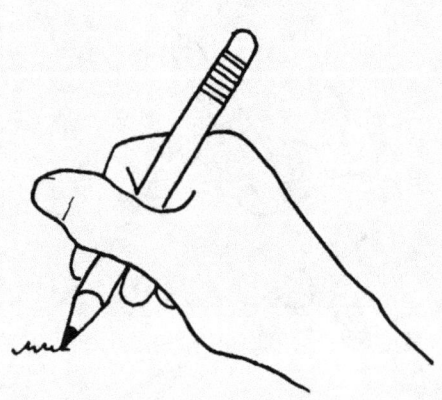

# THE CLARITY CONTRACT

_____

_____

_____

_____

_____

_____

_____

_____

_____

_____

_____

_____

_____

_____

_____

Date:                                    Signature:

_____        _____

# CHAPTER 9
## LEADERSHIP AS DAILY LEGACY

*"You don't need to become anyone else to lead powerfully. You already have what you need inside of you."*

—Dr. Tammi Fleming

## PURPOSE OF THIS CHAPTER:

This chapter is designed to help you reframe legacy as something you live—not just something you leave. It's about shifting from a pursuit of validation to a practice of impact, integrity, and presence. You'll explore the kind of influence you want to have in real time, and what it means to lead with love, consistency, and intention.

## How to Begin This Chapter

You've done the work to reclaim your voice, lead with clarity, and align with your purpose. Now, you'll reflect on what it means to lead in a way that shapes others—even when no one is watching.

Before you begin:

- Reread the letter in Chapter 9 of the book (Page 248). Let it settle.

- Think about a leader who left a lasting impression on you—what did they do consistently?

- These activities are meant to ground you in presence, not performance.

*Reflect honestly—this chapter is an offering, not an evaluation.*

# ACTIVITY 1:
# DEFINE YOUR LEGACY MARKERS

List five words or phrases you want people to associate with your leadership:

- 

- 

- 

- 

- 

*Now answer:*

- *Why do these matter to you?*

- *Are you embodying them now?*

- *What small shift would move you closer?*

(You'll find space on the next page to write.)

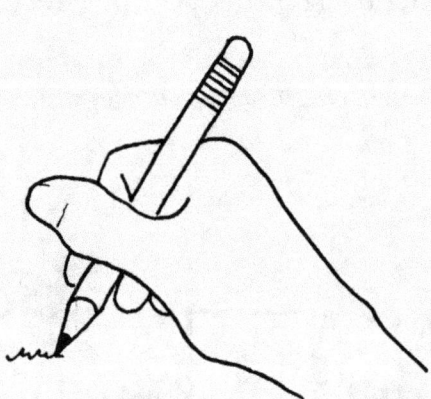

# ACTIVITY 2:
# DAILY LEGACY REFLECTION

For 3 consecutive days, journal your answers to:

- Who did I lead well today, and how do I know?

- In what ways did I show up with presence?

- What energy did I bring into the spaces I entered— and what energy did I leave behind?

## DAY 1

_____

_____

_____

_____

_____

_____

_____

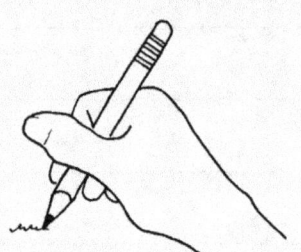

## DAY 2

_____

_____

_____

_____

_____

_____

_____

## DAY 3

_____

_____

_____

_____

_____

_____

_____

# ACTIVITY 3:
# WRITE YOUR "BECAUSE OF YOU" STATEMENT

Complete this sentence from the perspective of someone you've influenced:

"Because of you, I..."

Write 2–3 imagined versions of what someone might say five years from now because of how you led them today.

_____

_____

_____

_____

_____

_____

_____

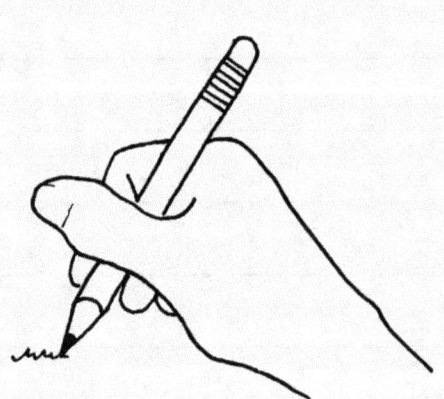

# ACTIVITY 4:
# CREATE YOUR LEADERSHIP INHERITANCE LIST

List the lessons, practices, or values you want to pass on:

- To your team

- To your community

- To your family

Circle the ones you're already modeling—and star the ones you want to be more intentional about.

- 
- 
- 
- 
- 
- 
- 
- 
-

# YOUR LEADERSHIP JOURNEY DOESN'T END HERE

You've taken time to pause, reflect, and grow through The Leadership Detour Companion Guide. That alone is powerful. But real transformation happens when reflection becomes practice—and when practice is supported in community.

If this guide helped you see yourself more clearly, name your truth, or reclaim your voice... don't stop here.

**Ready to Go Deeper?**

Here are a few ways to continue your journey:

**Book a Free 30-Minute Discovery Call**

Whether you're navigating a transition, facing self-doubt, or redefining success on your own terms, executive coaching can support your next breakthrough.

**Let's explore what's possible—together.**

**www.diamondconsultantsllc.com/schedule-time**

**Join The Executive Lounge**
 A private membership space for leaders ready to grow with intention. Get early access to resources, digital courses, book clubs, and honest conversations about what leadership really looks like.

**www.community.diamondconsultantsllc.com**

# EXPLORE FREE DIGITAL COURSES

Based on the core themes in this guide—emotional intelligence, executive presence, and leading from within.

**Start with The Leadership Compass**

To access the course, first join the Executive Lounge and then click the Learning tab.

**www.community.diamondconsultantsllc.com**

You've done powerful work. Keep going—because your legacy is already unfolding.

With purpose,

*Dr. Tammi Fleming*

# GLOSSARY OF TERMS

These terms appear throughout the Leadership Detour Companion Guide and are part of the leadership language we're reclaiming, redefining, and practicing. Whether you're new to these concepts or deepening your understanding, use this glossary to support your reflection and growth.

........................................................

| | |
|---|---|
| **ANCHOR / MIRROR / KEY** | Mentorship archetypes:<br><br>The **Anchor** grounds you with stability and wisdom.<br><br>The **Mirror** reflects truth and shows you who you are.<br><br>The **Key** unlocks doors or stretches your capacity. |
| **BELONGING** | A sense of being seen, valued, and included without needing to perform or prove your worth. True belonging means you don't have to erase parts of yourself to be accepted. |
| **BURNOUT** | A state of emotional, mental, and physical exhaustion caused by prolonged stress, overwork, or the pressure to prove yourself. Often a signal that boundaries or support systems need attention. |

| | |
|---|---|
| **COACHING PROMPT** | A thought-provoking question designed to challenge assumptions, deepen insight, and support personal transformation. Included at the end of each chapter section. |
| **EMOTIONAL INTELLIGENCE** | The ability to recognize, understand, and manage your emotions—and to recognize, understand, and influence the emotions of others. Includes five domains: self-awareness, self-regulation, motivation, empathy, and social skills. |
| **EMPATHY** | The ability to see and feel what others are experiencing, without assuming or fixing—just witnessing. |
| **EXECUTIVE PRESENCE** | The ability to project confidence, clarity, and credibility. More than appearance or tone—it's how you carry your values, voice, and visibility in a way that fosters trust and influence. |
| **LEGACY** | Not what you leave behind, but what you leave within others. Legacy is built in real time through your actions, presence, and impact—not reserved for the end of a career. |

| | |
|---|---|
| **MOTIVATION (INTRINSIC)** | Leading from purpose and values, not pressure or external validation. |
| **PROFESSIONALISM (REFRAMED)** | Traditionally rooted in conformity, this guide redefines professionalism as alignment between values and behavior—not emotional suppression or code-switching to fit in. |
| **RECLAMATION** | The act of taking back parts of yourself that were silenced, suppressed, or dismissed—especially in spaces where you felt the need to shrink. |
| **SELF-AWARENESS** | The practice of noticing what you're feeling, thinking, and believing in the moment—and how that influences your behavior. |
| **SELF-ERASURE** | The quiet habit of muting your voice, downplaying your ideas, or minimizing your needs to maintain acceptance or avoid conflict. |

| | |
|---|---|
| **SELF-REGULATION** | The ability to pause before reacting. It's not emotional suppression; it's emotional responsibility. |
| **SOCIAL SKILLS (IN EI)** | How you build trust, navigate dynamics, and communicate with clarity and care in real time. |
| **SOMATIC AWARENESS** | The practice of noticing how emotions show up in your body. Becoming attuned to your physical responses (like tension, shallow breath, or racing heart) is key to emotional intelligence and grounded leadership. |
| **THREE STORIES TOOL** | A reflection practice that explores three angles in a conflict or emotional moment:<br><br>• The story you told yourself<br><br>• The story the other person might tell<br><br>• The possible truth in between |

## ABOUT THE AUTHOR

Dr. Tammi Fleming is an executive coach, strategist, and author of The Leadership Detour: How the Unexpected Path Shaped My Success. With decades of experience across government, philanthropy, and nonprofit leadership, she helps leaders rise with clarity, courage, and conviction. As the founder of Diamond Consultants, LLC, she equips professionals to lead with purpose and presence. Tammi believes that leadership is not about performance—it's about transformation. This companion guide reflects her passion for helping others lead from the inside out.

www.diamondconsultanstllc.com